CONTENTS

Acknowledgements

The author and publishers wish to acknowledge, with thanks, the following photographic sources:

Barnaby's Picture Library pp 22, 62 bottom; BBC Hulton Picture Library pp 5, 6 bottom right, 7, 10, 11 right, 17 centre, 17 bottom, 21, 23, 29 bottom, 30, 31, 35, 36, 38, 41 top, 47, 48, 49, 50, 51, 52, 53, 54, 56, 58, 59 bottom, 60 top, 60 bottom, 62 top; Mary Evans Picture Library pp 6 top, 6 bottom left, 8 top, 8 bottom, 11 left, 13, 15, 17 top (Fawcett Library), 19, 29 top, 33, 34, 41 bottom, 43, 59 top, 61; The Heatherbank Museum of Social Work p 25; The Trustees of the Tate Gallery, London p 9.

The publishers have made every effort to trace the copyright holders, but if any have been inadvertently overlooked, they will be pleased to make the necessary arrangements at the first opportunity.

PREFACE

The study of history is exciting, whether in a good story well told, a mystery solved by the judicious unravelling of clues, or a study of the men, women and children whose fears and ambitions, successes and tragedies make up the collective memory of mankind.

This series aims to reveal this excitement to pupils through a set of topic books on important historical subjects from the Middle Ages to the present day. Each book contains four main elements: a narrative and descriptive text, lively and relevant illustrations, extracts of contemporary evidence, and questions for further thought and work. Involvement in these elements should provide an adventure which will bring the past to life in the imagination of the pupil.

Each book is also designed to develop the knowledge, skills and concepts so essential to a pupil's growth. It provides a wide, varying introduction to the evidence available on each topic. In handling this evidence, pupils will increase their understanding of basic historical concepts such as causation and change, as well as of more advanced ideas such as revolution and democracy. In addition, their use of basic study skills will be complemented by more sophisticated historical skills such as the detection of bias and the formulation of opinion.

The intended audience for the series is pupils of eleven to sixteen years; it is expected that the earlier topics will be introduced in the first three years of secondary school, while the nineteenth and twentieth century topics are directed towards first examinations.

WOMEN IN SOCIETY 1860-1928

Joyce Hodgson

Former Head of History, St. Joan of Arc Comprehensive School,
Rickmansworth, Herts.

MACMILLAN

First published 1989

Published by
MACMILLAN EDUCATION LTD
Houndmills, Basingstoke, Hampshire RG21 2XS
and London
Companies and representatives
throughout the world

Printed in Hong Kong

British Library Cataloguing in Publication Data
Hodgson, Joyce
Women in society 1860–1928.——(History
in depth).
1. Great Britain. Society. Role of women,
1850–1939
I. Title   II. Series
305.4′2′0941
ISBN 0–333–46358–7

1 'WOMAN, THE COMPANION OF MAN'

The year is 1919; the place, Stepney, in the East End of London. A woman is walking down the street, knocking on each door that she comes to. Her name is Annie Barnes and she is hoping to get elected as a local councillor. She knocks on one particular door and it is opened by a woman. Annie herself tells us what happened next:

I said: 'We're canvassing on behalf of the Labour Party.'

'Oh, I don't know anything about it,' she said. 'Just a minute, I'll get my husband.'

Then he came out and he said, 'Oh yes, I'll vote Labour, but I won't vote for the woman.' There were three candidates for each ward, you see, and the other two were men. He said that with me standing there.

'I'll vote for the men, but not for the woman. I'm not in favour of women taking part in anything. Let them stay at home. That's all.'

'Thankyou very much,' I said.

Annie Barnes: *Tough Annie*, 1980

ward: area represented by a local councillor

The brief scene described above sums up what this book sets out to explore. On the one hand we have the husband, who represents the traditional view of women's place in society, and his wife, who seems to agree with him. But knocking on their door is Annie Barnes, former suffragette and future Stepney councillor. She is one of the women who have left the shelter of the home and have stepped out into the wider world. Our task is to find out how and why women like Annie took that step.

'I'm not in favour of women taking part in anything,' the man on the Stepney doorstep said. 'Let them stay at home.' In 1860 most people, women as well as men, would have agreed with him. This may sound strange since at the time Britain's head of state was a woman, but in fact Queen Victoria herself thought the same way. The Victorians believed that men and women had different natures and were therefore suited to different roles in life. This was put very clearly by a writer of the time:

A Victorian middle-class couple. Note that the husband is seated while the wife stands

eminently: above all others

The man's power is active, progressive, defensive. He is eminently the doer, the creator, the discoverer, the defender . . . his energy [is] for adventure, for war and for conquest.

John Ruskin: *Sesame and Lilies*, 1865

Women, he goes on to say, have different gifts. They introduce peace and order into their surroundings and they give encourage-

5

A husband discusses with his wife the amount of money she has spent at the milliner's (hat-maker's)

ment to the creators and the defenders. These qualities suit them for the role of homemaker:

> *And wherever the true wife comes, this home is always round her . . . . The stars only may be over her head, the glow-worm in the night-cold grass may be the only fire at her foot, but home is wherever she is; and for a noble woman it stretches far round her, better than ceiled with cedar or painted with vermilion, shedding its quiet light for those who else were homeless.*

ceiled: with a ceiling of . . .

John Ruskin, as above

Above: *women lived under the authority of their fathers and then of their husbands*

Left: *a soldier and his family painted in about 1900. Compare this picture with the one on page 9 painted by George Hicks in 1863. How much had things changed in 40 years?*

As this last quotation shows, women were often seen in an idealised way. Men had to go out into society; they had to make a career for themselves and play their part in running the country. Ruskin points out that while they were doing these things, they might be tempted to be dishonest and proud and could commit all sorts of other sins. Women were sheltered from these temptations; it was as if the home was a sanctuary where all the right values were respected, and women were the guardians of the home. They were thought to be more virtuous than men and morally superior to them.

Physically and mentally, however, women were regarded as inferior to men. Usually this was just taken for granted, but sometimes people tried to give reasons for it. In a lecture to the Anthropological Society in London in 1869, James MacGrigor Allan said:

> . . . women are unwell . . . on average, two days in the month, or say one month in the year. At such times, women are unfit for any great mental or physical labour. . . . In intellectual labour, man has surpassed, does now, and always will surpass woman for the obvious reason that nature does not periodically interrupt his thought.
>
> Quoted in *Suffer and Be Still*, ed. M. Vicinus, 1972

Elizabeth Garrett's oral examination in Paris. She was one of the women who challenged society's idea of 'respectable' female behaviour by studying to become a doctor

A correspondent writing to *The Fortnight* in 1874 made the same point, and Dr Elizabeth Garrett answered him by saying that female servants still coped with the same heavy work load when they had a period as when they did not. But the idea persisted that, in Queen Victoria's words, women were a 'poor, feeble sex'. Because of this, it

Mill-girls in Yorkshire are given good advice about saving up for marriage. What do you notice about the way the man in the picture is drawn?

A French cartoon about the place of women in society. No doubt about who wears the trousers here!

was thought that a woman needed someone stronger and wiser to take care of her – in other words, a man. For a married woman, this would be her husband; for a single woman, it would be her father or, if he was dead, a brother.

In order to be able to protect and guide their womenfolk, the men had certain rights over them. Some of these rights were simply a question of accepted practice, of what was generally done. Harriet Martineau, for example, was 27 when her father died. She helped to support her family by writing, and on one occasion she wanted to go to see her publisher about a book that she had planned. Her mother would not let her go, however, until her brother had approved of the visit.

Men also had certain rights in law. In common law it was said that 'husband and wife are one person and that person is the husband'. One result of this was that any property that a woman might inherit or any money that she might earn belonged in law to her husband. For example, when Mrs Garrett Fawcett had her purse snatched in a London street, the youth who did it was charged with stealing 'from the person of Millicent Fawcett a purse containing £1.18s.6d., the property of Henry Fawcett'. If a husband ill-treated his wife, she could not bring a case against him, since in the eyes of the law they were 'one person'. Indeed, the law regarded a man's wife and children as his belongings, which meant that if she left him she could be legally compelled to return. If they agreed to live apart, custody of the children was automatically given to their father unless they were under seven, in which case the mother could ask to be allowed to keep them with her until they reached that age.

There is no evidence that Victorian husbands spent all their time beating their wives and ill-treating their children, and there were certainly families where it was the wife who was in charge, no matter what the law might say. But the fact remains that women had very little freedom of choice about what they did with their lives. Ruskin had spoken of the home as a sanctuary. The actress Florence Farr, on the other hand, said 'Home is the girl's prison'. In the years between 1860 and 1928 many women came out of the home and began to play a part in the larger world beyond. This process of change is called the 'emancipation' of women, for to emancipate people is to set them free. We shall be looking at what happened through the eyes of some of the women involved, although of course we can only mention a small number of those who made a contribution. The changes were most noticeable in three areas: the school, the workplace and the home.

Using the evidence

A

'Woman's Mission: Companion of Manhood', by George Elgar Hicks

B This is a description of life in a middle-class household at the turn of the century:

My father seemed to me a very important person and this . . . [was] largely due to the general attitude of the womenfolk of the house towards him. In my mother's opinion, everything he did was right. . . . She considered it right that the life of a wife, that the life of all the women in the household, should revolve around its male head. Nurse, the maids, and even Lizzie the cook, accepted this attitude without question, and everything went smoothly.
Enid Starkie: *A Lady's Child*, 1939

1 In source **A** the man has received news that someone in his family has died. Since he is so upset, we might expect him to be sharing his feelings with his wife. Is he doing this?

2 Describe how the man and his wife are standing. What is the artist telling us about men and women by painting them in this way?

3 Look again at source **B**. How did Mrs Starkie's attitude towards Mr Starkie affect Enid's view of her father?

4 What reasons would you give for Mrs Starkie's attitude towards her husband?

5 What impression do sources **A** and **B** give you of relations between men and women at this time? How much do you think things have changed since then?

GIRLS AT SCHOOL

2

Schools for young ladies

A girl with four brothers older than herself is born under a lucky star.

This is how Mary Vivian Hughes begins her book, in which she describes her childhood in the 1870s. Like many middle-class girls she sometimes found her life rather dull, but her brothers did help to liven it up:

My father's slogan was that boys should go everywhere and know everything and that girls should stay at home and know nothing. Often the boys must have been sorry for me, and one day when I exclaimed, 'How lovely it must be to go on top of a bus!', Dym first laughed at the idea and then suddenly said, 'I say, Barney, let's take her.' Barnholt, of course, was only too ready, and I rushed to get my things on before something could happen to stop us. If I had been asked to a royal ball I couldn't have been more excited.

M.V. Hughes: *A London Child of the Seventies*, 1934

On another occasion, the boys decided to visit all the schools for young ladies in the area. They told the headmistresses that as their mother was not very well they were making enquiries on her behalf about sending their young sister to school. The headmistresses

A cartoon by Cruikshank entitled The scholastic hen and her chickens. *Schools were expected to produce young ladies whose only career was to be marriage*

Noses to the North!

received them very politely, treating them to wine and cakes, and they all thought it a good joke. But it was not quite so funny when one of the headmistresses called on their mother, to see why the young lady had not yet come to school.

In fact, Mary's mother had decided to give her lessons at home. Girls' schools at this time did not offer much in the way of an academic education. This was because people took it for granted that girls would get married and that they did not need an education in order to be wives and mothers. Indeed, mothers often warned their daughters that gentlemen would not marry ladies who appeared to be 'bookish', and we have already seen that Mary Hughes' father said that 'girls should . . . know nothing'. But there were certain skills that people thought were ladylike, such as playing the piano or painting in water colours. It was these skills that most parents wanted their daughters to be taught at school or by a governess at home.

Using the evidence

A In 1864 Parliament ordered a Schools' Inquiry. Here is what one of the officials, James Bryce, had to say about a girls' school which he regarded as typical:

catechisms: books with questions and answers

The list of school books which they used – mostly catech-isms upon all subjects, including Greek and Roman history and geography and nearly every branch of science – would fill a page, and yet not one could do the simplest sum in the

Queen's College, London, was opened in 1848 to provide training for future governesses, but for a long time parents continued to prefer teachers who would pass on 'ladylike' skills rather than an academic education

Before 1870 there were some voluntary schools for working-class children, such as this one run by the Ragged Schools' Union. Note the women teachers and the way the pupils are seated in class

11

by rote: by heart

addition of money, or answer any question in English grammar except in the words of the book that she had got by rote. Further examination of the pupils would no doubt have disclosed equal ignorance on other subjects, but the mistress seemed so much distressed by the children's performance that I gave over questioning them.

Quoted in P. Gosden's book, *How They Were Taught*, 1969

B In the following passage Mary Hughes describes how her mother educated her at home:

... mother would summon me to her side and open an enormous Bible. It was invariably at the Old Testament, and I had to read aloud the strange doings of the Patriarchs.... After the reading, every word of one verse had to be parsed. After this effort mother usually gave her-self up to her hobby of water-colour painting, seated at the end of the dining-room table, while I carried on by myself with a little reading, sewing, writing or learning by heart, in the offing. Every now and then I would come to the surface with a question about the meaning of a word, or a bit of hemming that needed pressing down, or a bit of French poetry to be 'heard'.... My English history was derived from a little book in small print that dealt with the characters of the kings at some length. I learnt how one was ruthless alike to friend and foe, and how another was so weak that the sceptre fell from his nerveless grasp. I seemed to see it falling. The book had no doubts or evidence or sources.... My dislike of sewing was as nothing to my hatred of sums. This was the correct word, for I never did anything but addition. Mother's arithmetic was at a level with the White Queen's, and I believe she was never quite sound about borrowing and paying back, especially if there was a nought or two in the top row ... if the weather turned out tempting, my mother would dismiss all idea of lessons and take me out.... Such times were the best part of my education, for my mother had had a richly varied... life... and her matured wisdom became part of me.

M.V. Hughes: *A London Child of the Seventies*, 1934

to parse: to analyse the grammar

White Queen: a character in Lewis Carroll's book, *Alice Through the Looking Glass*

1 In source **A**, James Bryce complains of the girls' ignorance. What examples does he give of this?

2 Later on in his report he says that when one of these girls has grown up and become a mother: '... she finds that her education has not made her any fitter ... to educate and govern her children ... she is just where her mother was and her children suffer for it.' Explain what he means by this statement, using his criticisms of the school that he visited to help you.

3　In source **B**, how does M.V. Hughes show that she is aware of the limitations of the book from which she learned her history? Can you find any evidence that, in spite of this, as a child she enjoyed reading the book?

4　What advantages of being educated at home are shown in this passage?

5　Mr Bryce and Mary's mother seem to disagree about a mother's ability to educate her children at home. Having looked at the evidence, which point of view do you find yourself most in agreement with and why?

The new schools

In 1882 young Mary Thomas – she became Mary Hughes after her marriage – went to school. It was a very special school called the North London Collegiate. We have seen that many parents felt it was unnecessary to give their daughters an academic education because they were going to become wives and mothers. But it was also

In 1897 a proposal to give women degrees at Cambridge was defeated, since it would also give them the right to vote on matters of university policy. It was 1948 before women got degrees on the same terms as men at Cambridge

generally believed that girls were not capable of understanding academic work; arithmetic, for example, was thought to be too difficult for the female mind. The headmistress of the North London Collegiate, Miss Frances Buss, was determined to prove that girls were just as intelligent as boys. She thought that the best way of doing this was to give them the same sort of education as their brothers. At her school the pupils learned arithmetic, geometry and algebra; they had lessons in history, geography and Latin and also learned some science.

Miss Buss also wanted to show that women were not fragile little creatures who needed a big, strong man to protect them. This is illustrated by one of the stories which Mary tells about her time at the school. At assembly one day she noticed that her neighbour looked unwell. Mary helped the girl to leave the room as quietly as possible, but afterwards she was called before the headmistress:

'Why did you take that girl out?' she thundered.

'She fainted. What else could I do?'

'You meant well, my dear, no doubt, but you must never allow a girl to faint.'

When I looked my surprise, she added: 'Once I was in church with a pewful of girls. I noticed that one of them looked like fainting. I leant across to her, shook my fist at her and said: "You DARE faint." And she didn't.'

M.V. Hughes, as above

One cannot help feeling that it would have taken a very brave girl indeed to faint under the nose of an irate Miss Buss!

Mary sometimes found all the rules and regulations at the school rather tiresome, but on the whole she seems to have enjoyed her time there. She even writes about the examinations with enthusiasm:

Among the minor pleasures of life few can equal the excitement of being presented with a fresh examination paper, when you feel at home with the subject....

Probably not many pupils nowadays would share Mary's feeling that an examination paper is one of 'the . . . pleasures of life'. But we have to remember that, at the time that she was writing, public examinations were still quite a novelty. In 1857 Oxford University had introduced a system of 'local examinations' which could be taken by school-leavers, and in the following year Cambridge had done the same. In 1865 Cambridge allowed girls to take these examinations and in 1870 Oxford followed suit. So Mary and her friends felt that they were taking part in an important new breakthrough.

Many people were impressed by the work that Miss Buss was doing and schools similar to the North London Collegiate were set up in various parts of the country. However, there were some differences between them. Most of these 'high schools', as they were usually called, did not offer physics or chemistry because they could not afford the laboratory equipment that these subjects demanded. Instead, they tended to concentrate on biology and botany. Nor did they all have the same aims as Miss Buss. The constitution of Manchester High School, for example, certainly does not speak of the equality of the sexes. It says that girls should be educated so that:

meet helps: companions

> *... they may become intelligent companions and associates for their brothers, meet helps and counsellors for their husbands and wise guides and trainers for the minds of their children.*
>
> Quoted in C. Dyhouse's book, *Girls Growing Up*, 1973

Nevertheless, these new schools slowly changed the expectations of both parents and pupils and opened up new horizons. Once girls had received the same sort of education as their brothers, and had sat the same examinations, it was natural that they should also think about going on to university. In 1878 King's College and University College, London, started accepting women students. They were allowed to sit the examinations at the end of their course and, if they did well enough, they were awarded degrees in just the same way as men. By 1895 most other British universities, including such old-established ones as Edinburgh and Durham, were also allowing women to take degree examinations.

Another area of further education that women were fighting to get into was medicine. Elizabeth Blackwell, in the United States, was the first woman to qualify as a doctor, and Elizabeth Garrett was inspired by her example to try to do the same thing in Britain. However, she was only able to gain admission to the Society of Apothecaries, whose members provided basic medical care; in order to obtain a degree in medicine she had to go to university in Paris. In 1870 she returned to this country and joined forces with Sophia

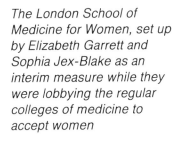

The London School of Medicine for Women, set up by Elizabeth Garrett and Sophia Jex-Blake as an interim measure while they were lobbying the regular colleges of medicine to accept women

Jex-Blake, who had been forced to abandon her medical studies in Edinburgh because of the hostility of the lecturers and the male students. Largely as a result of the efforts of these two friends and a few men who supported them, women were admitted to medical schools from 1880 onwards. Eleven years later there were 101 women doctors at work in Britain.

Elementary schools

The sort of education described so far in this chapter was, of course, only available to girls from the middle or upper classes. The fees at the North London Collegiate were quite low by comparison with other schools, but at £15 a year they were still beyond the reach of most parents, since the average national wage at this time was less than £1 per week. There were some schools for working-class children, run by voluntary organisations, but they were not found in every area and even where they had been set up girls were often kept at home so that they could help with the housework or look after the younger children.

Things changed when the Education Act of 1870 was passed. The Act said that in areas where there were no voluntary schools, a School Board must be elected. The Board would then set up and run a local school. This Act worked so well that by 1880 Parliament was able to make it compulsory for all children to attend school between the ages of five and ten. Here is how one woman who went to a Board school in London in 1900 remembers it:

The room held thirty-six desks; with two girls at each desk, seventy-two girls must have been in the one class. The desks did not open and the seats were attached. . . . We were given a pen with a nib which had to last a week. Books, too, were given out for each subject and collected and put in a cupboard when the lesson finished. We learned spelling, writing, reading, history, geography, arithmetic and nature study.

Grace Foakes: *My Part of the River*, 1974

You will notice that Grace only talks about the girls in her class. This is because in big towns there were separate schools for girls and boys. In areas where there were fewer children this was not possible, but even in mixed schools boys and girls entered the building by different doors, they had different playgrounds and sat on opposite sides of the classroom. The reason usually given for this was that it was necessary to protect the girls from the rough behaviour of the boys!

On the whole, the pupils all received the same education. There was, however, one exception to this: the girls were given special lessons in housework, laundrywork and cookery, usually while the

Above: *a school which specialised in teaching laundrywork, in about 1900. Pupils are being shown how to iron shirt collars and cuffs*

Right: *a drawing lesson, in about 1900. The pupils probably copied a picture drawn on the board by the teacher*

Right: *a geology lesson, held on the Icknield Way in 1913*

boys were learning science. In 1923 there was a Parliamentary Enquiry into this 'differentiation of the curriculum', as it was called. It had been suggested that the real reason for teaching girls housewifery was so that there would be a good supply of servants for middle-class families. But on the whole the Enquiry found that most people approved of the arrangement. Grace and her friends liked it, too, but not for the same reasons as the members of the Enquiry:

> . . . we were taught to sweep, dust, polish, make beds and bathe a life-size doll. We had great fun on this course, for it was held in a house set aside for the purpose, and with only one teacher in charge we were quick to take advantage when she went to inspect some other part of the house. We jumped on the beds, threw pillows, drowned the doll and swept dirt under the mats. This was the highlight of the week, the one lesson that we never minded going to.
>
> Grace Foakes, as above

If you look at the three pictures of classes in elementary schools, you will see why Grace and her friends were so glad of a chance to let off steam.

Questions

1   Compare the pictures of the elementary school classes with Grace Foakes' description of her school. What evidence can you find in them to support her description? Do they give you any additional information? Do they in any way give you a different impression of these schools from the one that Grace gives?

2   What are the main differences that you notice between Board schools and the school that you go to?

For the girls in the elementary schools there was no hope of sitting the sort of examinations that Mary Thomas and her friends had sat, nor of going on to university. This would have meant attending a fee-paying secondary school. From 1902 onwards some local education authorities did offer scholarships to pupils wishing to continue their education after the age of 14. However, there were not many such scholarships available and, even if a youngster did gain one, the child's parents would still have to make considerable financial sacrifices. For example, they would lose the money that the young person could have been earning. Also, although the scholarship would cover the school fees, there would still be other expenses to be met, such as the cost of the uniform, games kit and so on. Parents might be willing to make such sacrifices for a son, but they would be very unlikely to do so for a daughter, who would probably 'only get married' at the end of it all. If this was true of the cost of secondary schooling, it was even more true of further education. It was not until 1925 that local authority grants became available to students in further education.

Through education women gained literacy, numeracy and some knowledge of the world around them. They would need all these things if they were going to play a part in the wider world outside the home. But education also introduces us to new ideas and leads us to ask questions. It may cause us to ask why our life is the way it is and whether there is anything we can do to change it. So it is not surprising that many people saw education as the first vital step on the way to women's emancipation.

Using the evidence

A   *A cartoon published in* Punch *in 1872*

THE COMING RACE.

Dr. Evangeline. "By the bye, Mr. Sawyer, are you engaged to-morrow afternoon? I have rather a ticklish Operation to perform—an Amputation, you know."

Mr. Sawyer. "I shall be very happy to do it for you."

Doctor Evangeline. "O, no, not *that!* But will you kindly come and Administer the Chloroform for me?"

THE COMING RACE.

1872.

B This is an extract from a speech made by Sophia Jex-Blake, in which she describes her experiences as a medical student at Edinburgh University. All had gone well at first, but in order to qualify as doctors, she and the other students had to do some practical work in a local hospital. Mrs Jex-Blake explains what happened when the male students heard that the women were going to be allowed to do practical work:

. . . from that day the conduct of the students was utterly changed . . . those who had hitherto been quiet and courteous became impertinent and offensive; and at last came the day of that disgraceful riot, when the college gates were shut in our faces and our little band bespattered with mud from head to foot. It is true that other students . . . came indignantly to our rescue, that by them the gates were wrenched open and we protected in our return to our homes. . . .

Quoted in J. Horowitz Murray's book,
Strong-minded Women, 1984

C *The performance of domestic duties is her proper office – the management of her household, the rearing of her family, the economizing of the family means, the supplying of the family wants.*

Samuel Smiles, writing in 1843

1 Look at source **A** and take note of the date. How is the woman dressed? What does this suggest to you about the cartoonist's attitude to women doctors?

2 Why do you think the cartoon is entitled *The Coming Race*?

3 Look again at source **B**, and then say what sort of work a medical student might be expected to do in a hospital. Why did many people think that this was not the sort of work that should be done by 'ladies'?

4 Apparently not all the male students were opposed to the idea of women qualifying as doctors. How did the two groups of men behave on the day of the 'riot'? If you had been a passer-by at the time, whose side do you think you would have been on and why?

5 In source **C**, what does the author say is a woman's real job in life?

6 What views do you think Samuel Smiles might have had about the education of girls?

WOMEN AT WORK

3

In the late nineteenth century many new jobs became available to women. We are going to look at these through the eyes of certain women living at the time. Their names are imaginary, but what happened to them is based on fact. Let us imagine that it is the year 1900. It is a cold but sunny morning in November and you are walking down the High Street on your way to school. Suddenly you hear a cheerful shout:

'Hello, young 'un! Is it cold enough for you?'

It is Ellen Brown, the sister of your best friend. She started work last week as a maid at Dr Allison's. Now she is on her knees, scrubbing the front steps of his house, the steam from the hot water in her bucket rising into the frosty air. There are more women in domestic service than in any other type of work; in 1851 there were just over one million of them and by 1901 this number will have gone up to two million. Ellen would have liked to have got a position with Sir William and Lady Calstock, on the other side of town. They have ladies' maids, parlour maids and nursery maids, in addition to a cook, kitchen maids and a scullery maid. Dr Allison and his wife can only afford to employ a cook and a nanny as well as Ellen, so she has to work a lot harder than she would have done at Calstock Manor. But it is better than being a hotel maid and Ellen hopes that in a few years' time she may have learned enough to get a job as a cook somewhere, for cooks are better paid than maids.

Hotel maids in 1892. The different uniforms that they wear show that they do different jobs. What do you think is in the can held by the woman on the left?

You wave to Ellen and go on your way. The post office and general store is open and you remember that you still have a half-penny left from your pocket money, enough to buy two ounces of humbugs. As you go into the dark little shop the familiar smells come to greet you: the fragrance of sweets and beeswax polish mixed with the fumes of paraffin and the gaslights. There are no other customers and the postmistress, Miss Victoria Tutbury, comes from the back of the shop to serve you. Miss Tutbury and her sister inherited the shop from their father. It was not unusual for women to serve in these little general shops which were used by the poorer people.

In the past, wealthier families had always gone to specialist shops where the assistants were men. They were expected to have expert knowledge about the goods that they sold. For example, in a tea and coffee merchant's, they would have to mix tea and roast and grind coffee to suit the taste of individual customers. However, in the second half of the nineteenth century there was a great expansion of the retail trade. This was partly due to the new industrial processes, which produced goods in greater quantities and more cheaply than before. Also, although many people were still very poor, the standard of living was rising, especially for skilled workers, so there were more goods available and more people wanting to buy them. In order to exploit this situation, a new type of shop appeared: the department store. The most famous of these stores were in the West End of London, but many others were set up all over the country. The older shops had provided a specialised service to a small number of pat-

Between 1861 and 1911 the number of female shop assistants went up by 319 per cent, while the number of male assistants went up by only 118 per cent

rons, while the department stores sold all kinds of goods and were mainly interested in attracting customers and making as much profit as possible, so they were quite happy to employ women as they could be paid lower wages than men. Many women found the idea of working in these shops more attractive than going into service.

Miss Victoria Tutbury is a small, plump woman with red cheeks and dark hair done up in a bun. When she has weighed out the sweets on the shining brass scales, she winks at you. Then she glances into the room at the back of the shop where you can just see her sister sitting. Miss Victoria puts her finger on her lips and, taking two more sweets from the big glass jar, pops them into the paper bag for you.

Like the women working in the department stores, Miss Mary Tutbury is doing a job that is new to women. In fact, it is new to everyone. You can see her now, in the room behind the shop, sitting at a telephone switchboard. The first telephone exchange in Britain only came into operation in 1879. Not many people in your town have telephones yet, so Miss Mary can handle most of the work herself. If there is a telegram to be delivered and Miss Victoria is busy in the shop, Miss Mary asks the butcher next door to send his errand boy to deliver it.

Another invention which has opened up new job opportunities for women is the typewriter. The first of these machines suitable for use in offices came onto the market in 1873. Traditionally, office work had been done by men, but since typing was a new skill, women were able to secure this sort of work without too much difficulty. In

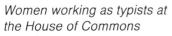

Women working as typists at the House of Commons

fact, employers often preferred to use women operators on both typewriters and telegraphic equipment. They believed that women had greater manual dexterity than men and could cope better with work that required them to remain sitting down for a long time. From working at the typewriter, women managed to move into other kinds of office work and by this year of 1900 there were 100 000 women employed in Britain as shorthand typists and secretaries.

Your grandmother does not approve of all these newfangled jobs. Going into service was good enough for her and she often grumbles about the women who are working in shops and offices. She reckons that they are trying to 'rise above their station in life'. In fact, they are not rising very high. In the shops, the managers of the various departments are nearly always men, and in the post office and telegraph companies the supervisors are men. Female secretaries work for male bosses. But at least women have a greater choice of jobs in 1900 than they had in 1860, and the new jobs do offer some variety and experience of responsibility.

You thank Miss Victoria for the sweets. Putting one in your mouth, you leave the shop and run the rest of the way to school. You do not want to be late for fear that your teacher, Miss Biddy, might use her cane on you. Your class reckons that Miss Biddy is much too fond of her cane – and of the multiplication tables. This morning you are just in the middle of chanting the nine times table and wondering if you can smuggle a sweet to your neighbour without Miss Biddy noticing, when a senior girl comes in with a note from the head-master. The district nurse has come to inspect everyone's head for what she calls 'unwelcome visitors'. You and your friends are glad to have your dull lesson interrupted, and you all like Nurse Farley. When she does have to give a child one of the dreaded bottles of special shampoo to take home, she always makes a joke of it so that the person does not feel embarrassed.

Miss Biddy and Nurse Farley are two more examples of women who have benefited from new job opportunities. Of course, women have been involved in teaching and nursing for many years, but now these jobs have to be done in a new way. In the old voluntary schools, where teachers had only been expected to deal with the 'three R's' – reading, writing and arithmetic – teacher training had not seemed necessary. It is true that there was the pupil–teacher system, under which pupils who wanted to become teachers could serve a sort of apprenticeship, but very often they were used simply as child minders. When the national network of elementary schools was set up in the 1870s and 1880s, it was felt that a more organised and thorough training should be given to future teachers. Universities and local authorities began to set up training departments for people who wanted to teach in elementary schools. Their courses were usually organised on a non-residential basis. This was a help to women, since parents who were unwilling to allow their daughters to

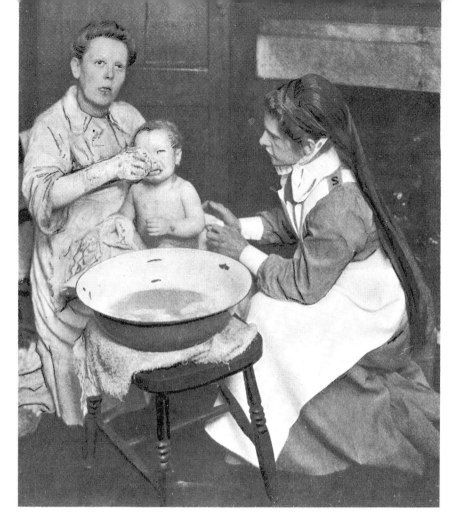

A 'slum-nurse' at work. It was partly through the work of such women that the middle classes became aware of working-class living conditions. But these nurses were often resented as 'busybodies' by the people they tried to help

go away to college might more easily be persuaded to let them attend day courses. Some colleges were also set up for women with degrees who wished to train as secondary school teachers, although there was less demand for this because secondary schools were fee-paying and so there were fewer of them.

Just as schools had changed a lot since 1850, so too had hospitals. In the past, medical treatment had been fairly primitive and conditions on the wards unpleasant. As a result, not many people wanted to work in them and the women who did become nurses were people who had usually failed, for one reason or another, to get work elsewhere. These women often spent their off-duty hours getting drunk or working as prostitutes, both on the streets and in the hospital wards. But medical practice was changing rapidly. Hospitals were introducing new equipment, such as hypodermic syringes, and new antiseptic procedures. They needed to find nurses who could understand and operate these new forms of treatment. Nurses are the only working women who receive your grandmother's approval.

'Nurses were a different kettle of fish when I was young,' she often says. 'That Miss Nightingale, now, she's changed things. Ladies, even, some of these hospital nurses are nowadays.'

Most people would agree with your grandmother in giving Florence Nightingale the credit for reforming the nursing profession. There were others working in this field, including the founders of the hospital at Kaiserwerth in Germany, where Miss Nightingale herself spent some months in training, but it is true that she did more than anyone else to bring the issue to public attention. In 1860, when she returned from nursing the soldiers in the Crimean War, she opened the Nightingale School of Nursing at St Thomas's Hospital in London. The students at the school were carefully chosen and one young woman was expelled for 'walking out' with a medical student. This incident showed how determined Miss Nightingale and her fellow reformers were to change the public image of nurses.

Nurse Farley did her training at the Nightingale School, but she thought that a hospital job would not give her the independence that she wanted, so she decided to work in the community. Again, it was Florence Nightingale who had helped to set up the first of these community nursing schemes, at the request of a Liverpool businessman. Similar schemes were set up around the country and in 1889 their members joined together to form the Queen Victoria Jubilee Institute. The members of the Institute were known as 'Queen's Nurses'. Nurse Farley is very proud of this title and she enjoys her work a great deal. Every month she has to send a written report to an inspector at the Institute, but on the whole she is able to make her own decisions and organise her own time.

Miss Farley is not what your grandmother would call a 'lady', for her father was the foreman at the local iron foundry, but certainly there are more 'ladies' working than ever before. In the early part of the nineteenth century, middle-class families took a pride in the fact that their womenfolk did not need to go out to work. The only job that was acceptable for a 'lady' was governessing, and people always thought that she would only do this if she was driven to it by necessity. But the census returns from 1851 onwards show that there were more women than men in the population; by 1901 the difference was nearly one and a half million. Moreover, this trend was most noticeable in the middle class. As a result, there was a growing number of unmarried middle-class women who either did not have male relatives to support them or who preferred to be independent. Thus, the increase in the number of jobs available to women coincided with an increase in the number of women looking for work.

At last your school day ends, and you and your friend walk home together. The streets are cold and when you get in you are glad to see that there is a pan of soup heating on the stove. You sit by the stove, watching your mother as she cuts slices of bread to go with the soup and thinking about all the working women that you have met today – Ellen, the Misses Tutbury, Miss Biddy and Nurse Farley. You probably think to yourself that, of all of them, it is your mother who works the hardest – and she does not even get paid for it!

Using the evidence

A *Miss Margaret Bondfield, assistant general secretary of the union [the National Union of Shop Assistants], was appointed a witness before the Truck Committee of 1907. Her evidence was based on her own experience: fines, she told the Committee, would amount to as much as 5s. out of wages of 10s. a week.... 'For addressing a customer as "miss" instead of "madam" ... not using string or paper with economy ... wrongly adding up bills ... [the fine] would be 3d..... In my experience of business life, the mistakes which occur are mainly due either to nervousness or overwork, for which fines are absolutely no remedy whatsoever.'... The living-in system, affecting some 400,000 out of 750,000 shop assistants, was equally condemned. 'I was put into a room with a woman of mature age who led a life of the most undesirable kind.... There was another girl in the same room who was suffering from consumption.'*

living-in system: workers lived in hostels run by the employers

consumption: tuberculosis

Barbara Drake: *Women in Trade Unions*, 1920

B This is an oral account of what it was like to work as a cook in a doctor's house in the 1920s. It was recorded in 1987.

There was an advert. in the paper and I applied and Mrs Frank [the doctor's wife] came down to see me. I suppose she wanted to see what sort of home I came from, how we talked and all that. They already had one child, Ann, and she would have picked up all the speech. We had one girl there that Mrs Frank sacked because she spoke very badly and Ann was picking it up from her.

spoke very badly: had a strong local accent

Every time I gave my notice in they used to give me more money to get me to stay. Ann came into the kitchen once and was rude to me and I told her to go out of the kitchen. About half an hour later she came back and apologised and I said 'That's all right, Ann. Off you go now.' And she said 'Daddy said that if I apologised you might let me stay.' But I said 'That's your punishment for being rude. You can come back tomorrow.' I daresay I was hard. But I won't have a child be rude to me. I think she called me a silly cow – where she got it from I don't know, but I thought to myself 'That's not good enough for me.'

We used to work there, used to work until twelve o'clock at night and then get up at six o'clock in the morning and start all over again. There was a gardener's cottage at the bottom of the garden and I used to sleep there with another girl and the other girl, she used to get so cold, she used to come into bed with me.

C ... 'the young lady in business' ... refuses to exchange her black uniform and her title of 'miss' for the cap and apron and name without a handle of the domestic servant.

Clementina Black: *Dictionary of Employments Open to Women*, 1898

1 Explain in your own words the criticisms made in source **A** of either the custom of fining staff or the living-in system.

2 After 1918 it became more difficult to get servants. Can you find any evidence of this in source **B**?

3 Which aspects of the job described in source **B** might put a woman off the idea of going into service?

4 Source **C** tells us that if a woman became a shop assistant her uniform would be a black dress and she would be called 'Miss'. What does the source say would happen if she went into service? Why do you think this might make her prefer to work in a shop?

In the late nineteenth century there were still jobs for women in the traditional areas of employment, although the number working in agriculture declined rapidly, partly because agricultural labourers' wages had gone up during the Golden Age of Farming (1850–70), so women no longer needed to work in the fields to supplement their husbands' incomes. This was followed, from about 1875, by the agricultural depression when fewer workers of either sex were required. Industry, however, continued to offer work to women. Some were employed in the manufacturing sector, particularly the textile mills of Lancashire; others worked in the service industries, such as laundries.

In the years between 1914 and 1918 many women worked hard to support the war effort. They worked in munitions factories and military hospitals. They even took over many of the jobs that were normally done by men: they drove buses, there were women 'doormen' at Selfridge's department store in London, and in the country women went back to working in the fields. Once the war was over, however, the employers took back their male workers. In 1921 there were almost exactly the same number of women in work as there had been in 1911, and they were doing much the same jobs: secretarial work, teaching and nursing.

However, women's experience of work during the war had a lasting effect. Sometimes they had been paid the same rates as men for the work they had done, but more usually they had received two-thirds of a man's wage. Even so, this was a lot more than they were used to being paid and it gave them a standard to aim at in subsequent pay negotiations. Also, the women who had worked in

Right: *a woman making matchboxes at home. Many women contributed to the family income by working at home, especially in rural areas. They were the lowest-paid workers in the country*

Below: *match girls at work in 1895. The strike by these women was one of the most influential actions taken by low-paid workers, although they were not members of a union at the time*

traditionally 'male' occupations, where unions were strong, had seen at first hand how working conditions and rates of pay had been improved by unionisation. The results of this were quickly seen. In 1919, for example, dressmakers, who were notoriously overworked and underpaid, formed a union and managed to negotiate a national minimum wage of 28s. for a 48-hour working week. Probably the most important result of women's war work was that it changed the way the public saw them and the way they saw themselves. They had shown that they could cope with all kinds of work and all sorts of situations. People's attitudes do not change overnight and women were still a long way from having equal status with men, but the war certainly played a part in their emancipation.

Women helping with farm-work during World War I

orthodox: generally accepted

Using the evidence

Here are a number of ideas that were put forward to explain women's apparent lack of interest in trade unions before 1914:

A *Trade unionism means rebellion and the orthodox teaching for women is submission.*
  Miss O. Ford, Leeds Society of Workwomen, quoted in Barbara Drake's book, *Women in Trade Unions*, 1920

B *One reason which, I think, tends to keep women out of the union is the lack of training which women have in managing such an organisation as a trade union. . . . When they have been educated sufficiently to do the work of negotiating with employers, and also in keeping accounts, I think women will be far better organised.*
  Mr Gee, General Union of Textile Workers, as above

C *I find that women as a body do not attend to the branch business as well as the men. . . . When a man has done his day's work he becomes free, and that is not so with women.*

Mr W. Thorne, Gasworkers' and
General Labourers' Union, as above

D *There are yet other and greater difficulties in organizing women. . . . First I would place their impatience. . . . They are unstable to a degree . . . their uncharitableness to each other is probably the most biting and disintegrating force which works against their solidity.*

Mr Keegan, Birmingham Pen Makers, as above

E

'Employment' of women? *A cartoon, dating from about 1870, on the subject of women working in offices*

F This extract is taken from a report on the metal industry drawn up by the Women's Trade Union League. Women had worked as chain and nail makers since the eighteenth century, but now the unions complained that women were taking men's jobs and were helping to cut men's wages.

[The investigators] were obliged to admit the charge of cutting men's wages. They deplored the low rates of 3s. and 4s. a week, which undermined the men's standards.

Quoted in Barbara Drake's book, as above

G Here is an extract from a speech made to the Trades Union Congress in 1877 by Mr Broadhurst, secretary of the TUC's

31

Parliamentary Committee. He said that he and his colleagues looked forward to the day when:

. . . their wives should be in their proper sphere at home, instead of being dragged into competition for livelihood against the great and strong men of the world.

Quoted in Barbara Drake's book, as above

1 Think about the explanations given in sources **A–D** in the light of what you know about women's lives at this time. Can you think of any other explanations? Using your own words, list the explanations, starting with those that you think were the most important and ending with the least important.

   You might like to do this in a group discussion. Here are two questions to start you off:

   What do you notice about the people who are putting forward these explanations? Does their identity in any way affect your view of what they say?

   What skills would a working woman need in order to run her home and perhaps do a job outside the home as well? In the light of this, what do you think of the ideas put forward in source **B**?

2 Look at source **E**. What do you think is the artist's opinion of women office workers? How does he make this view clear to you?

3 Look again at source **F**. How did the fact that women were accepting low wages 'undermine the men's standards'?

4 Use the sources quoted in this section to explain why relations between male and female workers in industry were strained. How reasonable do you think the men's attitudes were?

WOMEN AT HOME

4

Daily life

We have seen that between 1860 and 1928 it was gradually becoming possible for women to make more choices in life, thanks to better education and more job opportunities. But when they got married, most women gave up work – indeed, in the 1920s it was made compulsory for women teachers, nurses and civil servants to resign when they married. What was life like for these women and how much freedom did they have once they became full-time wives and mothers? In order to answer these questions we shall look first at a typical day in the lives of two women from different backgrounds.

We start with 'Mrs B'. We meet her in a survey which was carried out in Lambeth between 1909 and 1913 by the Fabian Women's Group. The Group investigated families that had an income of about £1 a week, a reasonable wage for a working man at that time. We can imagine Mrs B living in one of the typical houses of the area. These were rented out, with at least two families living in each house. There were five or six rooms, which were quite small, and in order to save space there was no landing at the top of the stairs. Instead, the steps continued upwards until they met the end wall of the house; they did not have a handrail and one of the investigators noted that it was not unusual for parents carrying young children in their arms to

A typical lower-working-class home in the late nineteenth century.

A cartoon from Punch. *The caption read: 'What's up wi' Sal?' 'Ain't yer erd? She's married agin!' A writer of the time said that when men were reproached for assaulting their wives, their most common reply was: 'May I not do what I will with my own?'*

trip and fall down the stairs. Here is the description of Mrs B as she appears in the survey:

> *This woman is tall and would be good-looking if her figure were not so much misshapen. . . . She has quantities of well-washed hair, and good teeth; but her face is that of a woman of fifty. She is thirty-eight. . . . She once went for a fortnight's change to the seaside. The visitor asked her, when she came back, what she had most enjoyed. She thought for a considerable time and then made the following statement: 'I on'y 'ad two babies along of me, an' w'en I come in me dinner was cooked for me.'*
>
> Maud Pember-Reeves: *Round About a Pound a Week*, 1913

The survey goes on to tell us that Mrs B has eight children and that her husband works at night as a labourer in a printing works. Every day she gets up at 6.45 a.m. and breast-feeds the baby, who is six months old. Then she calls the older children and gets them ready for school. As far as washing is concerned, the investigator says: 'Girl of ten can do for herself. Boy of ten can do all but his ears.'

They have bread, butter and tea for breakfast before leaving home. At 8.45 a.m. Mrs B feeds the baby again and gets the three younger children up and dressed. Her husband comes home at about this time and she cooks him a rasher of bacon for his breakfast. Then he goes to bed and Mrs B washes up the breakfast plates and cups. When she has made the beds, she settles the children down for a little nap while she goes out to buy something for dinner.

The older children come home for their midday meal, then return to school. At 1.45 p.m. Mrs B gives the baby another feed; she welcomes these feeding times because they give her a chance to sit down for a quarter of an hour. The investigator describes Mrs B's afternoon work: 'Sweeps kitchen, scullery, passage, scrubs them, cleans grate; three babies to mind all the time.' Also, of course, she has to try to keep the children quiet so that Mr B can sleep. At about 4 p.m. the older ones come back from school and she gives them their tea before cooking a meal for her husband. When it is ready she calls him. He eats his dinner, then leaves for work. She washes the children and puts them all to bed. She sits mending the family's clothes before going to bed herself at about 10.30 p.m. She shares her bed with the three younger children and wakes twice in the night to feed the baby.

Questions

1 Why do you think Mrs B's face 'is that of a woman of fifty'?

2 The investigator notes that she has 'well-washed hair'. What does this tell you about her? Can you find any similar evidence in the description of her day?

3   What were the two things that Mrs B enjoyed about her holiday? Why do you think she enjoyed these things particularly?

4   Look again at the description of the house and of how Mr and Mrs B spent their day. What effect do you think these living conditions would have had on their relationship?

We tend to forget, in these days of labour-saving devices, just how hard Mrs B and her friends had to work if they were to keep their homes clean and tidy. Here, for example, is a description of the weekly washday:

> *My mother, a coarse apron made from a sack round her and a square of mackintosh pinned over her chest, rubbed each piece with 'Sunlight' soap, giving an extra rub to the very dirty parts. . . . After the whites were washed, they were put in the copper to boil together with more soda. They were continually stirred with the copper stick and kept boiling for half an hour. The whole place smelled of boiling washing and steam. After this, they were lifted out . . . and left to drain. . . . Mother struggled to the sink with the bath of dirty washing water and emptied it. Then it was filled with cold water and placed under the wringer. The washing was rinsed once and put through the wooden rollers. If the weather was fine, it would be hung out to dry.*

copper: tank in which water was heated
soda: often used as cheap substitute for soap

Grace Foakes: *My Part of the River*, 1974

Of course, in wet weather the washing would have to be hung up indoors until it was dry. It must all have been quite a nuisance in those cramped little Lambeth houses, but the housewives tried not to let it get them down. One woman tells how she began to realise that she and her husband were drifting apart, because her mind seemed to be totally occupied with looking after the house and children. So she bought some copies of famous books which were being published

Washing day in the Scottish Highlands. Compare the methods they are using with the picture of the English housewife at her washtub on page 33

An advertisement for an early washing machine. Note the price and the remarks made by those who recommend it!

WASHING-DAY REFORM.

HARPER TWELVETREES'

UNRIVALLED LABOUR-SAVING

VILLA WASHER,

Wringer and Mangler combined, £5 5s. (Cash Price, £4 15s.), or without Wringer and Mangler, £2 15s. (Cash Price, £2 10s.)

Does the Fortnight's Family Wash in Four Hours, without RUBBING or BOILING, as certified by thousands of delighted purchasers.

The Rev. J. ROBINSON, Great Sampford, Braintree, writes—"With the aid of the servant, aged 14, the Fortnight's Family Washing for six in family is done in four hours."

Mrs. CHARLES PAMMENT, St. Saviour's Villa, Bury St. Edmunds—"Our Fortnight's Family Wash, which formerly occupied from 8 A.M. till 8 P.M., is now done in three hours, and the copper fire is out five hours sooner than it used to be."

Carriage paid; free trial; easy instalment payments, or ten per cent. cash discount.

New Illustrated Catalogue, 48 *pages, post free, from*

HARPER TWELVETREES, Laundry Machinist,

80, FINSBURY PAVEMENT, LONDON, E.C.

at one penny each and propped one up in front of her whenever she was scrubbing the weekly wash.

By 1900 many working-class men felt that their wives should not go out to work unless it was absolutely necessary. But if they were to live on the husband's wage alone, the wives had to be good financial managers. Seebohm Rowntree, investigating the poorer families of York in 1901, gives us the example of Mrs Smith who was keeping house on £1 a week:

Old garments, cast off by some wealthier family, are sometimes bought from the ragman . . . and made up into clothes for the children. Mrs Smith said that she once bought a pair of old curtains from the ragman for 3d. She cut out the worn parts and then made curtains and short blinds from the remainder sufficient for all the windows in her house. She regularly pays 6d. a week for sick clubs, 4d. for life insurance, and 3d. per week into the clothing club.

B. Seebohm Rowntree: *Poverty: A Study of Town Life,* 1901

1 Explain what the 'ragman' did.

2 How do you think the sick club and clothing club operated? Can you think why Mrs Smith might prefer to save through clubs rather than keeping the money at home?

3 How do you think Mrs Smith would have felt as she hung up the curtains that she had made?

Mrs B's life was typical of most working-class wives. But what was daily life like at the opposite end of the social scale? Let us take as an example an imaginary woman, Lady B of Westminster. She would get up at about 8 or 9 a.m. and would spend the morning dealing with household affairs. She might have to see the cook about a dinner party that she was giving at the end of the week. 'Do make sure the gardener knows that we shall want plenty of asparagus,' she tells cook. 'He made a dreadful fuss about it last time and we don't want to upset him again.' Then she has to see one of the maids who came back late last night, following her afternoon off. Lady B is a kindly woman so she does not dismiss the girl this time, but she does warn her that if she is late again she could lose her job. She also gives her some motherly advice about not letting any young man lead her astray!

In the afternoon Lady B changes into one of her best day dresses and goes to call on some of her friends. There are a lot of rules about paying calls, such as how often one should visit people and how long one should stay. Mrs Beeton, in her book of advice for young wives, includes this warning:

> *During these visits, the manners should be easy and cheerful.*
> *. . . Serious discussions or arguments are to be altogether avoided.*
> Mrs Beeton: *Household Management*, 1861

She does not give any examples of what ladies could discuss, but the weather is always a safe subject, and so are fashions and the royal family. If the lady of the house is out when Lady B calls, she gives the maid a printed card with her name on it. Every upper-class house has a silver tray in the hall where these cards are placed, so that the mistress can see who has called on her. Soon she must return the calls.

Lady B returns home and at 6 p.m. the children are brought to the drawing room by their nurse. They always enjoy this time with their parents, when they tell them what they have been doing during the day. The eldest girl is 15 and she is looking forward to the time when she will be allowed to leave the schoolroom and join her mother on her afternoon visits. She is already dreaming about the dances that

Children of an upper-class family come down from their nursery to see their parents and the dinner-guests

she will go to, waltzing round the room in the arms of some handsome young man, while her mother and the other ladies look on. Or perhaps she will meet the handsome young man at a friend's house, when she is invited for an afternoon's tennis. . . . But all too soon the gong sounds and it is time for her and her brothers and sisters to go, leaving their parents to have their dinner in peace.

Lord B is in the government and often Lady B has to give big dinner parties for important guests. This evening, however, he has arranged to meet some friends at his club. When he has gone, his wife gets on with a tea cosy that she is making. She does not enjoy this very much, but she has been asked to organise a sale of work in aid of the Church Missionary Society, and she feels that she must set a good example to the other ladies. She probably goes to bed at about the same time as Mrs B.

Using the evidence

The following extract describes visits made by an upper-class girl and her mother to villagers on their estate:

> [Mother] often took me with her to visit the village women in Swinbrook with small gifts of charity. Their poverty worried me

and filled me with uneasiness. They lived in ancient, tiny cottages, pathetically decorated with pictures of the Royal Family and little china ornaments. The smell of centuries of over-cooked cabbage and strong tea lurked in the very walls. The women were old, and usually toothless, at thirty. Many had . . . crooked backs, and other deformities associated with generations of poverty. Could these poor creatures be people, like us? What did they think about, what sort of jokes did they think funny, what did they talk about at meals? How did they fill their days? Why were they so poor?

Jessica Mitford: *Hons and Rebels*, 1960

1   The women described in this passage lived in the country. Do you notice any similarities between them and the urban poor, such as Mrs B of Lambeth?

2   What impression do you get of the author from this passage?

3   How do you think women of the upper classes felt about the working class, judging by this extract and the way 'Lady B' treats her servants?

4   Working-class women needed to be hard working, determined and good with money. What qualities do you think an upper-class woman needed in her daily life?

Children

On several occasions, Queen Victoria wrote to her eldest daughter about her views on marriage. In one letter, dated 20 April 1859, she recalls how she felt on the night before the princess's wedding:

> *. . . it is an awful moment to have to give one's innocent child up to a man, be he ever so kind and good – and to think of all that she must go through! . . . I said to Papa . . . 'After all, it is like taking a poor lamb to be sacrificed.'*

Quoted in J. Horowitz Murray's book, *Strong-minded Women*, 1984

Not surprisingly, Prince Albert thought that his wife was exaggerating. But what did the Queen mean when she referred to marriage as a sacrifice? Judging by her other letters, one of the things she was thinking of was the burden of frequent pregnancies. Even upper-class women found that their health was undermined by constant childbearing, and for working-class women there was the additional worry of how to bring up six or more children on a wage that was barely adequate for two or three.

To some people, family planning seemed to be the answer, although many others condemned this as immoral. There were practical difficulties about it, too. In law, a woman had no right to refuse her husband if he wanted sex, so most people felt that it was the man's responsibility to take the precautions. But condoms had unpleasant associations because a man would usually only wear one if he were going with a prostitute who might be carrying disease. So a 'good' husband, to a working-class woman, was one who did not 'bother' her too often; that was her only real protection against unwanted pregnancies.

It was difficult for women to protect themselves because, for one thing, most people did not talk openly about sexual matters. Girls were not told anything about menstruation. One young woman, whose parents were out for the evening when she started her first period, got her brother to send for the doctor because they were both convinced that she must be seriously ill. Women even went into marriage in total ignorance of what to expect. The experience that one woman had on her wedding night was typical:

Her husband, a kindly enough fellow, appeared before her in the bedroom, told her she looked pretty, and shortly afterwards said, 'You know what has to be done, so don't make a fuss.' But she had literally no idea what had to be done – nor did millions like her. All she had learnt was from one of her married sisters who had said, without further explanation, 'When the time comes, dear, try to think of something else. It's the only thing to do.'
Duncan Crowe: *The Edwardian Woman*, 1978

One cannot help feeling that this conspiracy of silence was as unfair on the men as it was on the women.

However, the average number of children per family dropped from six in 1860 to two in 1920, and one reason for this was certainly the spread of knowledge about methods of birth control. The decline in the birth rate was most noticeable in the upper and middle classes. This is not surprising, for even if working-class women were able to get advice, they still found it difficult to afford contraceptive devices. Their answer to the problem of unwanted pregnancies was revealed by one woman who had had four children in five years:

I confess without shame that when well-meaning friends said 'You cannot afford another baby; take this drug,' I took their strong concoctions to purge me of the little life that might be mine.
Quoted in *Maternity: Letters From Working Women*,
ed. M.L. Davies, 1915

The 'drug' that she refers to was one of the medicines that could be bought in any chemist's shop. They were supposed to be for women whose periods were irregular, but in fact their real purpose was to cause a miscarriage. If this failed, and the woman was desperate, she

40

Marie Stopes in 1953

might go to an abortionist. This was strictly illegal and in fact many people were prosecuted for obtaining or performing abortions. It has been calculated that in 1935 there were 68 000 abortions carried out in Britain, of which 512 led to the death of the mother. By that time, however, a number of family planning clinics had been set up around the country to give women information about methods of birth control. One of the first of these was started by Marie Stopes in Ladbroke Grove in London. Women had to be quite brave to go there as it was next door to a centre for unemployed men, whose favourite pastime was to stand outside the clinic and make rude remarks to the women as they went in and out!

Women and the law

As we saw in Chapter 1, in the early nineteenth century a wife's earnings and any property she inherited belonged to her husband in the eyes of the law. In 1870, however, the first Married Women's Property Act was passed, allowing wives to keep their own earnings. In 1882 a second Act was passed. This gave married women the right to inherit and bequeath most kinds of property and to claim the income from investments made in their names. These Acts affected middle-class women particularly. They felt that they had greater social status, now that they were allowed to own property. Also, it gave them more independence. They were not likely to spend their

A cartoon about the 'training' of husbands

money in ways that their husbands would consider unwise, but they could do so if they wished. In time this was bound to change the way husbands saw their wives and the way wives saw themselves.

It was not only the wife's income that had belonged to her husband. Their children were also seen as his property and, if the parents separated or divorced, it was he who would have custody of the children. In 1873 the Infants' Custody Act gave the mother the right to ask to keep any children under 16, although there was no guarantee that the courts would agree. As far as divorce itself was concerned, the Divorce Act which had been passed in 1857 remained in force until 1923. Under this Act, a husband could divorce his wife for adultery. A woman wishing to divorce her husband also had to prove that he had committed adultery, but in addition she had to produce evidence of some other offence such as cruelty or desertion or homosexuality. Apart from the fact that it made it more difficult for a woman to obtain a divorce, the main criticism of the Act was that divorce proceedings could only be brought in a crown court, which was very expensive. After much debate the law was changed in 1923. Under the new law, a woman could sue for divorce on the same grounds as a man and proceedings could be brought in the county courts.

Two other changes in the law reflected public attitudes to women during the second half of the nineteenth century. In 1864 the Contagious Diseases Act had made the police responsible for having prostitutes checked regularly for symptoms of sexually transmitted diseases, in towns where troops were stationed. Only women who were certified as healthy were allowed to work as prostitutes in these towns. There was a lot of public anxiety at the time about such diseases, and it was thought especially important to protect the armed forces.

Nevertheless, the Act aroused a great deal of opposition. Some people, of course, disapproved of prostitution and felt that giving the certificates of health was like licensing the women. But the main objections were raised by a campaigning group led by Josephine Butler. She condemned the Act as being unfair to women. Men were equally responsible for the spread of these diseases, but they were not to be inspected. Moreover, the examinations were painful and degrading for the women concerned, and some even claimed to have sustained permanent injuries as a result. Worst of all were the cases of women who had nothing whatsoever to do with prostitution but who were arrested by the police on suspicion and forced to undergo internal examinations.

In 1886 the Act was repealed. Important as this was, the real victory of Josephine Butler and her supporters was that they had brought this matter out into the open and forced people to think about the way women were being treated. Another significant change in the law was the abolition, in 1884, of the penalty of imprisonment

There was anger at this time about the hypocrisy surrounding prostitution. It was regarded as acceptable for a man to visit a prostitute, or even to keep a mistress, but the woman herself was a social outcast

for any woman who refused to have 'marital relations' with her husband. By this time the penalty had fallen into disuse, but the fact that MPs felt that it should now be removed from the statute book tells us something about the changing attitude of society towards women.

Question

Imagine that you are a middle-class man or woman carrying out an investigation into the lives of urban working-class women, at some time between 1873 and 1923. Write two pages from your diary, recording your experiences and your feelings about what you have seen. The pages may cover consecutive days or not, as you wish. Use the source material given in this chapter as an aid. Remember, this is not an official report but a personal account. You will probably want to write something about the differences between your life and the lives of the people you are observing. Do you get on well with them? What seem to you to be their greatest problems? A word of warning: once you have decided on the date of your diary, make sure that what you say fits in with that date.

Coursework assignment: women in education, 1865–95

This exercise enables the student to look more closely at an important topic, while developing skills which are required for examinations.

a) **Skill: selection, arrangement and presentation of relevant knowledge**
(i) Draw a graph showing any six events that helped or hindered the progress of female education during this period. Arrange them in chronological order, and position each one on the graph according to how much it promoted or delayed progress.
(ii) Choose four of the events that you have shown on the graph. Write about 50 words on each, explaining why you think it was important.

b) **Skill: understanding historical terminology and concepts**
(i) In two or three sentences, explain what you think someone who lived at this time meant when they called a woman a 'lady'.
(ii) What were the characteristics that would cause someone to be labelled 'working class'? Give examples to make your explanation quite clear.
(iii) Give the meaning of the following terms in the context of this period:
elementary school;
high school;
Board School.

c) **Skill: evaluation of source material**
Look again at Sophia Jex-Blake's description of the 'riot' at Edinburgh (see page 20) and then read the following:

> *The tension and antagonism produced by changes in girls' education is hard to understand unless we see that an elaborate system of . . . boundaries was being broken down . . . women were stepping from a different and non-competitive world, and thus were polluting the values of both the world they left – 'the home' – and the world that they entered. . . . Dr Matthew Duncan claimed that [receiving the same education as men] would result in women's reproductive organs being harmed.*
> Pauline Marks: *The Rights and Wrongs of Women*,
> ed. Oakley and Mitchell, 1983

(i) Explain what is meant by 'primary' and 'secondary' sources.
(ii) Pauline Marks is not just telling us what happened during this period. What else is she doing and how would you test whether what she says is reliable?

(iii) Write a paragraph on some of the advantages and disadvantages of primary sources. Use the Sophia Jex-Blake extract to illustrate your answer.

d) Skill: empathy

In a working-class family of the 1890s, the eldest daughter, who is 14, has just told her parents that her teacher thinks she should become a pupil–teacher.

Either write a dialogue in which the girl and her parents discuss whether or not she should take up this opportunity, *or* discuss the matter in the form of a letter written by one of the girl's parents to a relative, seeking advice. In either case, write about one and a half pages.

e) Skill: analysis of cause and consequence

Look again at the cartoon in Chapter 2 entitled 'The scholastic hen' and at the one in Chapter 3 entitled '"Employment" of women?'. Compare these with what you have learned about the old and new girls' schools (Chapter 2), the new job opportunities available to women (Chapter 3), and the daily life of middle-class women (Chapter 4).

 (i) How would you describe the way in which women are shown in these cartoons?
 (ii) Leaving aside the question of prejudice, can you give two other reasons why people might have had this view of women?
(iii) Give three examples of types of professional training open to women during this period. Why do you think that the pioneers of women's emancipation were so eager for women to receive professional training?

5

THE RIGHT TO VOTE

Do you know how many women MPs there are today? See if you can find out the exact number. It is very small compared with the number of men in the House of Commons. This fact is sometimes used to show that women in general are not interested in politics. If this is so, why did women campaign for the vote between 1860 and 1928? How did they think it would change the position of women in society, and were they right?

When we talk about women campaigning for the right to vote, most people think of the suffragettes, who were active around the beginning of the twentieth century. But in fact the campaign began much earlier. The Manchester National Suffrage Society, for example, was founded in 1867. ('Suffrage' means the right to vote, and those who believe in giving people the vote are called 'suffragists'. As we shall see later, some women took direct action in support of their claims and were nicknamed 'suffragettes' by the press.) The secretary of the Manchester Society was called Lydia Becker. She was a middle-class woman who did not want to live a life of leisure at home. She studied botany and astronomy and then wrote basic textbooks on both these subjects. She also corresponded with Charles Darwin, the scientist who had become famous for his ideas on evolution. In addition to her work for the Suffrage Society, she was elected onto the local School Board. She was asked to lay the foundation stone of a new school for girls in 1877, but when she arrived for the ceremony she was horrified to learn that the school was going to specialise in teaching cookery. She made a speech condemning this narrow approach to female education and said that in her view every boy in Manchester should learn how to 'mend his own socks and cook his own chops'.

Most of the members of the early suffrage societies were middle-class people like Miss Becker, but in the 1890s some working-class women became interested in the movement. Many of them also belonged to the Independent Labour Party, which had been started in 1893. One such woman was Ada Nield. She had left school at the age of 11, to look after her seven young brothers. When she was older she went to work in a factory in Crewe, making uniforms for the army and the police. She created quite a stir when she wrote to the local newspaper, expressing how she and many others of her class felt:

Cultivation of the mind? How is it possible? Those of us who are determined to live like human beings and require food for mind as well as body, are obliged to take time from sleep to gratify this desire.

Crewe Chronicle, 5 May 1894

to gratify: to satisfy

In 1914 a meeting about women's suffrage was attended by representatives from the USA and Europe. One of the British representatives, Mrs Fawcett, is second from the left in the second row from the front

In 1901 a petition asking for the vote and signed by 29 395 working women was presented to Parliament. Helen Silcock was one of the organisers of the petition, and she explained the reason why she believed in women's suffrage to some MPs who were sympathetic to the cause:

> *I represent the Association of Weavers at Wigan, which comprises between 800 and 900 women, all of whom are in sympathy with the movement. I consider it unjust that five millions of working women in this country are denied the right of assisting to make the laws which they have to obey.*
>
> Quoted in J. Liddington and J. Norris's book,
> *One Hand Tied Behind Us*, 1978

Questions

1 Why did Ada Nield think that it was important for people to read?

2 What problem did she say working people had when it came to reading?

3 Why did Helen Silcock think that women should have the vote? Do you agree with her reasoning?

4 Using the information you have been given about her, write a brief character sketch of Lydia Becker.

5 The petition of 1901 was organised by members of a trade union and both Lydia and Ada believed in the value of education. Do you think there is any connection between these facts and the support which these women gave to the suffrage movement?

It is interesting that the first suffrage society was started in Manchester, for the town had also been the birthplace of the Anti-Corn Law League, which was probably the most successful of all nineteenth-century pressure groups. The early suffragists wanted to follow the League's example of winning people over to their point of view by argument. Like the League, they printed pamphlets and organised public meetings. However, there was one difference: the suffragists invited women as well as men to speak at their meetings. This was very unusual and surprised the audience almost as much as it frightened the women who had to speak. One suffragist from Bristol later recalled:

It was evident that the audiences always came expecting to see some curious masculine objects walking onto the platform, and when we appeared, with our quiet black dresses, the whole expressions on the faces of the audiences would instantly change.

Quoted in J. Liddington and J. Norris's book, *One Hand Tied Behind Us*, 1978

Suffragists attracted attention to their campaign in all sorts of ways!

1   What do you think the speaker meant when she said that
    audiences expected to see 'some curious masculine objects'?
    Why would they expect this?

2   In your own words, explain why you think the attitude of the
    audience would have changed when they saw the speakers.

From 1869 women who were unmarried, and who therefore still
owned their own property and paid rates on it, were allowed to vote
in borough elections, and in 1888 they were given the right to elect
county councillors as well. In 1894 these rights were extended to
married women, although husband and wife had to qualify as rate-
payers on different properties. The Act of 1894 also said that women
who had the right to elect local councillors should be allowed to
stand for election themselves. But as far as general elections and
central government were concerned, women were still not enfranchised, that is, they still did not have the right to vote.

As the years went by, more and more suffrage societies were
founded around the country, and in 1897 they came together to form
a national union. Another important development was the foundation, in 1903, of the Women's Social and Political Union. One of the
leading members of the Manchester Society had been Dr Richard
Pankhurst; the WSPU was started by his daughter, Christabel, and
her widowed mother. They soon enlisted the support of Christabel's
sister, Sylvia, although her views sometimes differed from theirs.

*Cycling was a very popular
pastime. Women especially
found that it gave them a
feeling of independence*

A rally at the Royal Albert Hall in 1908. What does this picture tell you about the connection between women's education and the suffragist movement?

One example of this was when Sylvia accused her mother and sister of supporting 'votes for ladies' rather than 'votes for women'. They wanted women to be given the vote on the same terms as men, but at this time the right to vote was still based on a property qualification. It is true that the Parliamentary Reform Act of 1867 had widened the qualification a great deal, so that in the towns even the upper working classes could vote. But the unskilled workers were still too poor to qualify and so were agricultural labourers. Sylvia Pankhurst thought that all men and women should be enfranchised, regardless of their income, and this division within the Pankhurst family reflected the division of opinion within the suffrage movement.

By the time the WSPU was founded, however, many suffragists were angry and frustrated. After 40 years of peaceful campaigning they felt that they had achieved nothing and they were ready to follow Christabel Pankhurst, who was urging them to take more drastic measures, to break the law and get themselves arrested. This was such an unusual step for women to take, especially if they were well-brought-up young ladies, that it would be sure to get publicity for the movement. The publicity was even greater when the women refused to pay the fines imposed on them by the courts and served prison sentences instead.

Christabel Pankhurst had a great deal of charm and seemed able almost to hypnotise people into following her lead. The 'suffragettes', as they became known, began making public protests. They repeatedly marched to the Houses of Parliament, and one woman even poured a bag of flour over the Prime Minister from the public gallery of the House of Commons. This sort of behaviour certainly got the women arrested and attracted public attention, but it also

A typical demonstration in favour of votes for women. Note the different sorts of people taking part in the march

meant that they were often involved in physical confrontations with the police. Soon they found that they were being beaten up and subjected to other forms of assault:

> *One [policeman] gripped me by the thigh, and I demanded that he should cease doing such a hateful action to a woman. He said 'Oh, my old dear, I can grip you wherever I like today.'*
> Quoted in Brailsford and Murray's report,
> *Treatment of Women's Deputations*, 1911

After a while the suffragettes began damaging property. This was much easier than trying to break through a police cordon at the Houses of Parliament, and yet it still got them arrested, which was what they wanted. To begin with, they broke the windows of government buildings, but soon the action escalated, as Sylvia Pankhurst remembered:

> *In Piccadilly, Regent Street, Oxford Street . . . well-dressed women suddenly produced strong hammers from innocent-looking bags and parcels, and fell to smashing shop windows.*
> Quoted in Barbara Castle's book,
> *Sylvia and Christabel Pankhurst*, 1987

At first, this sort of action attracted a great deal of attention, but when it no longer made the headlines the WSPU had to find more and more extreme forms of protest. By 1913 they were no longer just looking for publicity, they were hoping to cause so much trouble that the government would be forced to give in to their demands. This was why they started a campaign of arson. Here are some examples of the damage that they did in the first few days of May 1913:

51

The funeral procession of Emily Davison, who died after throwing herself in front of the king's horse during the Derby in 1913. What other signs of suffragette extremism can you see in the photograph? What does it tell us about the attitudes of the police and the public towards the movement?

May 3	Ashley Road School, Aberdeen	Est. Value:	£400
May 6	St Catherine's Church, Hatcham	" "	£15,000
May 7	Bishop's Park stand, Fulham	" "	£200
May 10	Boot warehouse, Nottingham	" "	£1,600

Morning Post, 13 July 1914

Questions

1 What groups of people would be affected by the damage done to each of the four targets listed above?

2 Are you surprised that the suffragettes attacked such a variety of buildings? Give reasons for your answer.

3 What effect do you think these attacks would have on the attitude of the public towards the suffragettes?

In fact, this action did not persuade the government to surrender. Instead, ministers became more hostile than ever to the suffragettes. This was made very clear by the way the women were treated in prison. They claimed that they were political prisoners and were entitled to 'First Division' status, which carried with it certain privileges, such as being allowed books and visitors. However, the

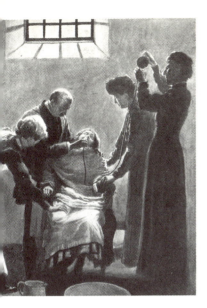

Forcible feeding of a suffragette in prison

Mrs Pethwick-Lawrence:
a wealthy supporter of the
WSPU

magistrates generally sentenced them to the 'Third Division', which was occupied by ordinary criminals. Once they were in prison the women would usually go on hunger strike, as a protest against this treatment. From 1909 onwards the prison authorities, with the approval of the government, introduced a programme of forcible feeding for women on hunger strike. This involved passing a tube through the nose or mouth, down into the stomach of the prisoner. Liquid food, usually milk, was then poured down the tube. The operation, as well as being painful and humiliating, was also dangerous, and there was such an outcry about it that in 1913 the practice was stopped. Instead, the government introduced the 'Cat and Mouse Act', as it was nicknamed by the magazine *Votes For Women*. Under the terms of this Act, a prisoner who went on hunger strike could be released and then, when she had regained her strength, she would be arrested and imprisoned again.

The women who went to prison suffered in other ways, too. It was especially difficult for working-class women, who had no servants to look after their families while they were away. Here is an example of what happened to one woman:

One of the Preston W.S.P.U., Mrs Towler, was imprisoned in Holloway after storming the House of Commons. Her husband was a [worker] in the weaving sheds and they had four sons: before she went down to Westminster she spent a week baking for her family, and left enough food to keep the five of them going for a fortnight. The women were sentenced to six weeks in solitary confinement in Holloway, but once the first two weeks were up Mrs Towler became extremely depressed at the thought of her family going hungry. In the end, her agitation became so great that Mrs Pethwick-Lawrence was asked to come and bail her out. Mrs Towler went back to Preston and lit her oven.

J. Liddington and J. Norris: *One Hand Tied Behind Us*,
1978

Questions

1 Make a note of where Mrs Towler was imprisoned, for how long and in what conditions. How do all these things help to explain why she became depressed?

2 What does this account tell you about Mrs Towler's personality?

By 1914 the suffragists had tried both persuasion and violence, but had still not obtained their objective. This was partly because the movement was divided over its aims and the methods that should be used to achieve them. Another reason was that the government of the day was faced with a number of other issues which it regarded as more important than women's suffrage. For example, it was trying to get the House of Lords to pass a Home Rule Bill for Ireland, as well as a budget that would help the poorer sections of the population at the expense of the rich. Economic problems had led to unemployment, rising prices and falling wages, which in turn had caused social and industrial strife. It is not surprising, therefore, that many MPs agreed with Winston Churchill, who thought it was 'a damnable nuisance' that MPs should be distracted by the question of votes for women when they should have been attending to more important things. The Prime Minister, Herbert Asquith, doubted whether most women really wanted the vote, and his doubts turned to hostility as the WSPU's campaign became more violent.

The caption on this photograph is typical of the generally unsympathetic coverage given to the suffrage movement by the press

THE SUFFRAGETTES' LATEST ABSURDITY: THEIR EJECTION FROM THE HOUSE OF COMMONS ON THE OPENING DAY OF THE SESSION, OCTOBER 23.

Thirty agitators for female suffrage were ejected by the police for disorderly conduct in the Lobby, and ten were arrested.

(See " Parliament," overleaf.)

The stalemate between the government and the WSPU was broken by the outbreak of war in 1914. Both Mrs Pankhurst and Christabel were in favour of the war, and they not only called off the campaign of militancy but urged all women to take up war work. In 1916 Asquith declared that women had contributed as much to the war effort 'as any other class of the community' and said that there was no longer any justification for denying them the vote. In 1918 an Act was passed enfranchising all men over 21 and all women over 30 who were householders or the wives of householders, or who were university graduates. The age qualification was introduced because women were thought to be more impulsive and changeable than men, so the vote was given to mature women only. Younger women, and women in the poorest classes of society, had to wait another ten years before they were given the vote on equal terms with men.

Why did women get the vote? Many people, like Asquith, linked their victory to their war work. Sylvia Pankhurst no doubt thought this ironic. She had said that the war was simply a struggle for territory between two power blocks, and had spent the war years working on behalf of the wives of private soldiers, who were often destitute. To her it must have seemed strange that a woman who had been called irresponsible for throwing a stone through a window six months earlier was now looked upon as a responsible citizen because she was making shells to kill German soldiers. But most people accepted Asquith's reasoning.

The government was anxious to make the point that it was not giving women the vote because of the campaign of militancy. After all, no politician likes to appear to be giving in to violence. The suffragettes had antagonised many people by their methods, but they had also kept the issue of women's suffrage in the news. The quiet but persistent efforts of the older suffrage societies, which continued to hold their meetings and publish their pamphlets right up until 1928, must also have had an effect. It would be difficult to prove how important each group's contribution was to the final result.

It was inevitable that women would get the vote sooner or later. We have seen how they were becoming better educated during this period. They were taking on more varied and more responsible work and they were gaining financial independence. They were sitting on local councils, school boards and the executive committees of trade unions. It would have been impossible to allow them to do all these things and to continue to deny them the vote. The war simply prompted politicians to act sooner rather than later. The proof of this came in 1928, when the Bill to give all women the vote at 21 was passed with hardly a voice being raised against it. In this way Parliament recognised how far women had come along the road to emancipation. Whether obtaining the vote has helped women to go further along that road is a question that you might like to discuss in class.

Using the evidence

A Annie Barnes describes her first encounter with the suffragettes:

I'd never really thought about that sort of thing. I'd been very quietly brought up. . . . Then, one day, something happened which really woke me up . . . there were four women on a cart speaking. That was unusual, to see women speaking.

The men in the crowd were just awful. . . . At one point a city clerk came right through the crowd up to the front and shouted at the women who were trying to speak, 'Go home and get on with the housework. Go and wash your dirty kids. You women are inferior to men anyway.' . . .

At the end of the meeting the four women asked all those interested to leave their names and addresses. . . . I went and gave my name and address. . . . I was a bit afraid. My parents would have died if they had known I was involved, though they thought the suffragettes had a lot of pluck.

Annie Barnes: *Tough Annie*, 1980

B This is an account of what happened when the police tried to arrest Sylvia Pankhurst again after she had been released from prison under the 'Cat and Mouse Act':

On one occasion there was a big meeting at Bromley Assembly Hall in Bow Road. . . . [Sylvia] was out on the Cat and Mouse Act at the time. . . . We all got to the hall, all

A woman exercising her right to vote in 1918

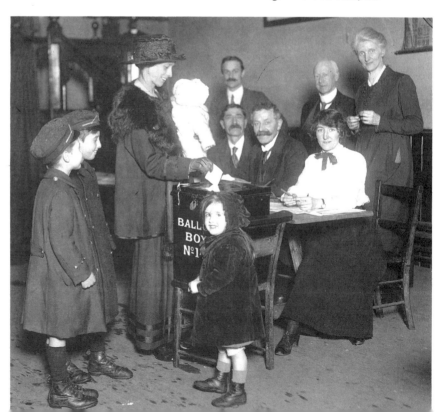

excited . . . and sure enough she appeared on the platform. . . . All at once these detectives got on the platform. As they were in plain clothes we didn't realise what was going on to begin with. But suddenly, people in the audience started shouting, 'Jump, Sylvia, jump, jump.' And they picked her up and threw her this way and that among the crowd, changing hats with her so that the police didn't know which one she was. Goodness, it was exciting!

Annie Barnes, as above

C Here is an extract from Christabel Pankhurst's defence when she was arrested for the first time:

We cannot make any orderly protest because we have not the means whereby citizens may do such a thing; we have not a vote; and so long as we have not votes we must be disorderly. There is no other way whereby we can put forward our claims to political justice. ·

Quoted in Andrew Rosen's book, *Rise Up, Women!*, 1974

1 Why would Annie Barnes' parents 'have died' if they had known that she was involved with the suffragettes?

2 What reasons would you give for the city clerk's remarks in source **A**? (You may find it helpful to think back to what you have learned about attitudes to women generally at this time.)

3 What did the audience do when they saw the police trying to arrest Sylvia Pankhurst? Can you think of two reasons why they might have behaved in this way?

4 What adjectives would you use to describe the atmosphere in the hall?

5 Do you think that the suffragettes were right to take direct action in order to try to bring about a change in the law? Are there any groups nowadays that act in the same way? Do you think we are ever justified in breaking the law? Give reasons for your answers.

6 a) Write a letter from a young woman to one of her relatives, explaining why she has just joined the suffragettes, and describing what she has been doing for the campaign and how she feels about it, *or* write a similar letter from the girl's brother, who admires what she is doing.

   b) Write a reply from the relative, who is opposed to the WSPU, giving reasons for his or her attitude. The relative may be against the whole idea of women's suffrage, or in favour of a non-violent campaign.

6 NEW WOMEN

When we try to imagine a woman of the 1920s she probably looks like Jessica Mitford's sister, Nancy. The oldest of four girls, Nancy was determined to be up-to-date, even though her father disapproved like parents all through the ages:

shingled: cut short

> *...Nancy at the age of twenty had her hair shingled. Nancy using lipstick....Nancy wearing trousers, Nancy smoking a cigarette – she broke ground for all of us, but only at terrific cost in violent scenes followed by silence and tears.*
>
> Jessica Mitford: *Hons and Rebels*, 1960

Not all women dared to wear trousers but they did wear much shorter skirts than their mothers had ever worn and these, together with their short hair, were signs of the more active life that women now lived.

Some people thought that the trousers were also a sign that women wanted to take over men's role in society. The same thing had been said in the 1890s, when there had been a lot of talk about the 'New Woman'. Cartoonists often depicted her wearing men's clothes and smoking, which was regarded as a typically masculine habit. This idea that women wanted to take over men's place in society was reinforced by the hostility that some women in the emancipation movement showed towards men. For example, Elizabeth Dean, a working woman from Manchester, once said about her father:

A girls' school of the 1920s

> *I always had it against him. My mother died when she was thirty-*

*Amy Johnson (1903–41).
She made a number of
record-breaking flights and
in 1930 became the first
woman to fly solo to
Australia*

*Miss Annette Ashley was
the first woman to be
elected to the Society of
Engineers, in 1925*

*eight; she'd had eight children and she died from the last one....
I always said that my father turned me into a suffragette.*

Quoted in J. Liddington and J. Norris's book,
One Hand Tied Behind Us, 1978

However, most of the women in the movement were happily married and many of the movement's supporters were men. For instance, one of the first people to draw attention to the unfair treatment of women in Victorian society was John Stuart Mill. He went so far as to say that the law made the married woman into her husband's slave. The second women's college at Cambridge was founded by a man, Henry Sidgwick, and Thomas Paterson worked with his wife Emma to convince working women of the value of unionisation.

Whatever the views of certain individuals might be, it would seem that the women's movement was not essentially hostile to men. But we have seen that people in the nineteenth century thought that women had different gifts from men and that they were therefore suited to a different role in life. Ruskin, among others, said that man was 'the creator, the discoverer, the defender', while woman was the homemaker. So if women wanted to be creators, discoverers and defenders as well, did that not mean that they were attacking men's position in society? One answer to this question might be that men and women sometimes have different approaches, but that does not mean that they cannot undertake the same tasks. It is just that they will each bring their own talents to the task and will tackle it in their own way – not better or worse, but differently.

If the women's movement was not an attack on men, what was it? It is difficult to give one answer to this question because there were so many different people in the movement, with different aims and

motives. In fact, even the word 'movement' is misleading, for it makes the people involved sound much more organised than they were. Some of the women mentioned in this book were not interested in the question of emancipation. Florence Nightingale, for example, steadfastly refused to have anything to do with any campaign for 'women's rights'. She said that being a woman had not stopped her from doing what she had set out to do and that this proved there was no need to change the law. There were other women who, while they had rather more sympathy with their down-

Emancipated women in 1929

Below: *even in 1925 there were still some 'schools for young ladies'. Here, the students learn the right and wrong way to pick up a handkerchief!*

trodden sisters, basically shared Miss Nightingale's approach to life. For them, emancipation was simply a question of being allowed to develop their talents and do the work that they wanted to do. Then there were women like Josephine Butler, who were more interested in the legal position and thought that men and women should be equal under the law. The suffragists went further, saying that if women had to obey the laws, then they should have a share in making them. For women like Annie Barnes, the struggle for women's rights was part of the greater struggle of the working class.

Using the evidence

A This extract describes one type of work done by women in 1928:

> *Market research was considered slightly above selling or office work; the pay was higher and it was the sort of employment that might 'lead to something better'. It attracted a mixed assortment; my co-workers, all women roughly between twenty-five and forty-five, were ex-chorus girls, wives of businessmen. . . . We travelled by train in teams of six or eight, herded by the supervisor, to manufacturing towns in the Midlands or North of England . . . . We were provided with elaborate forms to be filled out in the course of door-to-door interviews. . . . Interviewing for a breakfast food or household cleanser was fairly plain sailing, while a form dealing with a deodorant was likely to contain the question, 'How often do you find it necessary to wash under the armpits?'*
>
> Jessica Mitford: *Hons and Rebels*, 1960

A family picnic in 1928. Apart from the car, what other things would have been different about a family outing of the 1860s?

A mother with her two sons in 1928. Notice how the older boy is standing, in relation to his mother

B Here is another woman's memories of life in 1928, recorded in 1987:

Sometimes the girls would go out together in the evenings, to the cinema or a dance. But not to the pub – no decent woman would go to the pub. My father used to go there every evening for a glass and one night my mother said she was going, too. But my father said: 'If you walk in that pub, I'm walking straight out.' She didn't go. Very strict my father was. He wouldn't let me go to the dances. He said the boys only went there for one thing – to get their arms round a girl. When I'd been home for my afternoon out, I used to walk back to the place where I worked. It was only two streets away but my father always used to walk there with me, in case I was stopped by anyone. Twenty-two, I'd have been then.

What examples can you find in these two sources of women's greater freedom in 1928, compared with 1860, and of the limitations on their freedom which still existed? How important do you think these examples are?

How much had the women's movement achieved by 1928? An impressive start had been made. Even working-class girls received an elementary school education, and could then choose from quite a wide range of jobs. Once they were married they could usually afford to give up work, and had only two or three children to cope with, unlike their mothers who would probably have had six or eight. Girls from wealthier families could, if they wished, go on to higher education, and had an even wider choice of work. Women were even eligible for positions of political responsibility – the first woman MP, Lady Astor, was elected in 1919.

However, there was still much to be done. The women's movement was active again after 1945, and this produced further legislation to prevent discrimination against women, for example, in employment opportunities. But people's attitudes cannot be altered simply by changes in the law, and it is these attitudes that lie at the root of many of the inequalities that still remain. In the late eighteenth century Mary Wollstonecraft published her book *A Vindication of the Rights of Woman*. She was urged to write it by a man, Joseph Johnson. In it she said that while men must take some of the blame for the inequalities in our society, women were also to blame. And she said something that remains as true now as when she wrote it: that neither men nor women will be truly free until they see women's rights and men's rights as one and the same thing – the rights of human beings.

A working-class family in 1929

Skills grid

A Historical skills

1 *Using historical evidence*

	U 9	U 12	Q 18	U 20	U 28	U 32	Q 34	Q 37	U 39	Q 43	C 44	Q 47	Q 49	Q 52	Q 53	U 57	U 62
Comprehension of variety of sources			■														■
Distinguishing primary *v* secondary											■						
Extraction of information	■				■			■									■
Evaluation, recognising * fact *v* opinion																	
* gaps and inconsistencies						■											
* bias																	
* importance of origin and context						■											
Recognition of inference and implication in a source	■	■					■				■		■				■
Comparison of different sources based on relative reliability																	
Reaching conclusions on basis of this comparison																	
Judgement and choice between various opinions																	
Formation of overview and synthesis of one's own opinion												■					■

2 *Empathy*

Understanding events and issues from perspective of people in the past	■										■			■			

B Historical concepts

Cause and consequence		■								■		■					
Continuity and change					■												
Similarity and difference			■					■		■							■
Time, sequence and chronology																	
Interaction of individual with society	■					■									■		
Conflict and consensus																	
Historical vocabulary and terminology									■								■

INDEX

Numerals in **bold** denote illustrations